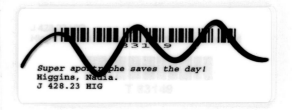

By Nadia Higgins • Illustrated by Mernie Gallagher-Cole

The Child's World®

Published by The Child's World®
1980 Lookout Drive • Mankato, MN 56003-1705
800-599-READ • www.childsworld.com

Acknowledgments
The Child's World®: Mary Berendes, Publishing Director
The Design Lab: Design and production
Red Line Editorial: Editorial direction

Design elements: Billyfoto/Dreamstime;
Dan Ionut Popescu/Dreamstime

ISBN 9781614732655
LCCN 2012932871

Printed in the United States of America
Mankato, MN
July 2012
PA02117

About the Author: Nadia Higgins is a children's book author based in Minneapolis, Minnesota. Nadia has been a punctuation fan since the age of five, when she first wrote "Happy Birthday!" on a homemade card. "I love punctuation because it is both orderly and expressive," Nadia says. Her dream is to visit Punctuation Junction someday.

About the Illustrator: Mernie Gallagher-Cole is a freelance children's book illustrator living outside of Philadelphia. She has illustrated many children's books. Mernie enjoys punctuation marks so much that she uses a hyphen in her last name!

All the punctuation marks in Punctuation Junction were doing their jobs. It was a quiet, orderly, and understandable day. The perfect day for a nap, thought Super A. She floated up to her bunk and yawned. Super A drifted off to sleep. Soon, she was having a wonderful dream.

"ALERT! ALERT! ALERT!"

"Huh? What?" Super A rubbed her eyes. Lights were flashing on her apostrophe alarm system.

"What on Earth?" The superhero frowned at what she saw. There was trouble at Pencil Elementary. The apostrophes were floating away. And were those commas filling in? No wonder it was so mixed up. This looked like a job for a superhero.

Super A turned her balloon to the jet setting. She took off for the school. "What happened?" she asked as she drifted down.

"It was the commas," Peter said. "They dared the apostrophes to touch the clouds."

"Then the apostrophes floated away!" Colin was crying.

"We just wondered if they could," Karen said.

"We tried to fix it," added Kiko.

"These things happen,"
said Super A. "Here." She
handed the commas a piece of
paper. "Study this while I'm gone." Then she turned her balloon
to the rocket setting. Super A shot into the sky.

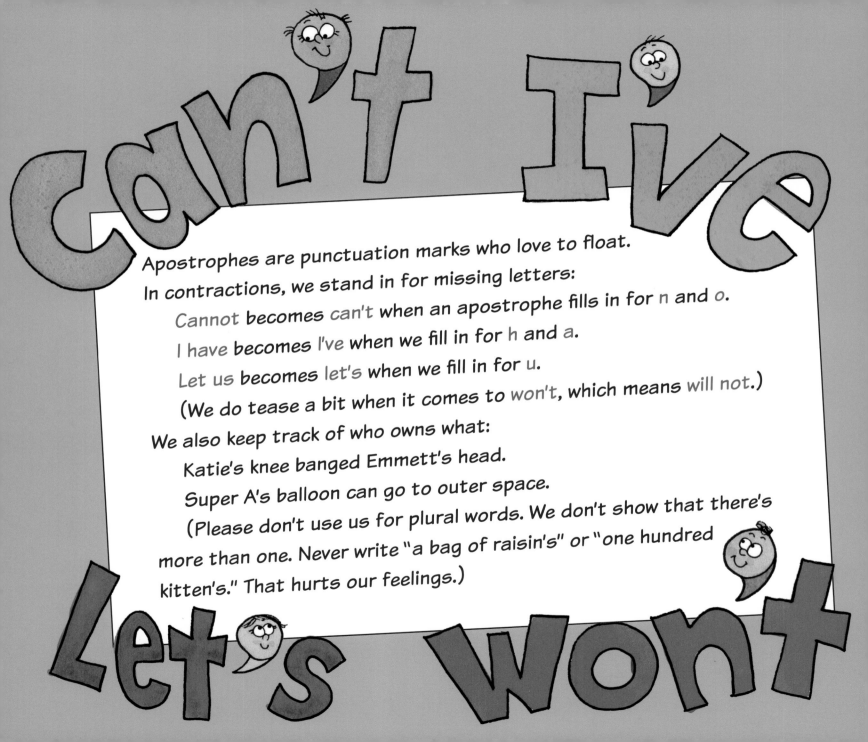

Apostrophes are punctuation marks who love to float.

In contractions, we stand in for missing letters:

Cannot becomes can't when an apostrophe fills in for n and o.

I have becomes I've when we fill in for h and a.

Let us becomes let's when we fill in for u.

(We do tease a bit when it comes to won't, which means will not.)

We also keep track of who owns what:

Katie's knee banged Emmett's head.

Super A's balloon can go to outer space.

(Please don't use us for plural words. We don't show that there's more than one. Never write "a bag of raisin's" or "one hundred kitten's." That hurts our feelings.)

Super A kept going up and up and up. Where were those apostrophes? How would she ever find them in outer space?

Zap! Zing!

With the force of *clear contractions*, and the power of *whose is whose*, Super A found her way.

She spotted the apostrophes on planet Zorp.
It looked like they were playing.

"Super A!" Arnie called out. "Come and play!
We've taught the aliens all about apostrophes."

"Why, that sounds just lovely," Super A said.
And she floated down to join the fun.

After many hours, it was time to go.

"Don't leave us!" the aliens cried. "Can't you, won't you, stay a little longer?"

"Hmmmmmm." Super A couldn't bear to see anyone looking so down.

"Why don't you join us?" she said.

The aliens perked up right away.

"We thought you'd never ask!"

"We'd love to!"

"Let's do it!" their leader said. "Everybody, pile into Lank's rocket."

Back in Punctuation Junction, the commas had gotten much better at filling in for the apostrophes . . .

. . . until the real apostrophes showed up with their guests.

"Apostrophes, won't you fix the banner, please?" Super A asked. Soon, everything was in place. Thanks to Super A, the day was again quiet, orderly, understandable—and so much fun.

PUNCTUATION FUN

The apostrophes have taken a short vacation to visit their alien friends. Can you fill in for them while they're gone? Add apostrophes to these sentences.

1. Lets fly away in a green rocket ship.

2. The aliens feelers almost popped Super As balloon.

3. Arnies toys need to be picked up, dont you agree?

4. Please dont add apostrophes to plurals such as kittens and raisins.

5. Wont you be my friend?

6. Dont you wish your friends were aliens?

7. Ive never seen so many stars in the sky!

8. Lets listen to my new favorite song by the Bad Apostrophes, "Dont Get Me Wrong."

DO NOT WRITE IN THE BOOK!

FUN FACTS

What a Surprise!

Sometimes a single word can end in *s*. For example, Charles is just one boy. You can still add an apostrophe and an *s* to show that Charles owns stuff: That's Charles's toy. You say "Charles's" like "Charlziz."

S-Apostrophe

When a word ends in *s* because it is plural (more than one), add an apostrophe but no *s*. What if two sisters share a room? You'd call it the sisters' room. In this case, "sisters'" sounds exactly the same as "sisters."

Hey, Baby

The apostrophe is one of the youngest types of punctuation in the English language. Most other punctuation has been in use since the 1600s. But the apostrophe didn't come into play until the 1800s.

What Time Is It?

Apostrophes just love it when a new hour begins. That's when people use one of their favorite words—o'clock. What time does school end? Three o'clock. Let's play!

DATE DUE

			PRINTED IN U.S.A.